To Anne and

With lots of love,

Jill xx .

Copyright © G. M. Stevenson, 2016
All rights reserved
The moral right of the author has been asserted

First Published in Great Britain in 2016 by
G. M. Stevenson,
Lisburn, Northern Ireland

ISBN 978-0-9935614-0-5

No part of this book may be reproduced or transmitted in any form
or by any other means without permission in writing from
the publisher, except by a reviewer who wishes to quote brief
passages in connection with a review written for insertion
in a magazine, newspaper or broadcast

The author has made every effort to clear copyright permissions,
but where this has not been possible and amendments are required,
the publishers will be pleased to make any necessary arrangements
at the earliest opportunity

A catalogue record for this book is available
from the British Library

Typeset in Times New Roman
Certain photographs used under
Creative Commons Zero (CC0) License.

Printed in Great Britain by
A1 City Print
32 Market Square, Lisburn, BT28 1AG

To dear Lynda,
without whom this book would
not have been written.

Acknowledgements

I would like to thank a number of people for their invaluable contributions to the production of this book.

Firstly, Paul Whittle for his I.T. expertise and all-round reliability. Also, Colin and Zoe from Waterstones booksellers, for their generosity with time, background knowledge and for generally keeping me on the right track.

Thanks to the staff at A1 City Print for their enthusiasm about getting this book out in time for it's launch and to Lynda Tavakoli, whose encouragement, kindness and insight helped me to believe in myself as a writer.

Finally, to all the characters throughout the book, without whom some of the stories and poems simply wouldn't exist.

Contents

Victoria's Child 9
The First Chapters 13
Everyday Love 17
This Life 21
The End of the Road 25
Charade 29
Haiku 33
Ending 35
Letting Go 39
The Parting of the Veils 43
Fallout 47
Loss 51
Autumn 55
Searching for Home 57
Home 61
Portmore 65
Frozen in Time 71
Acts of Love 75
The Fairies' Curse 79
(A Prayer For) A Perfect Death 83

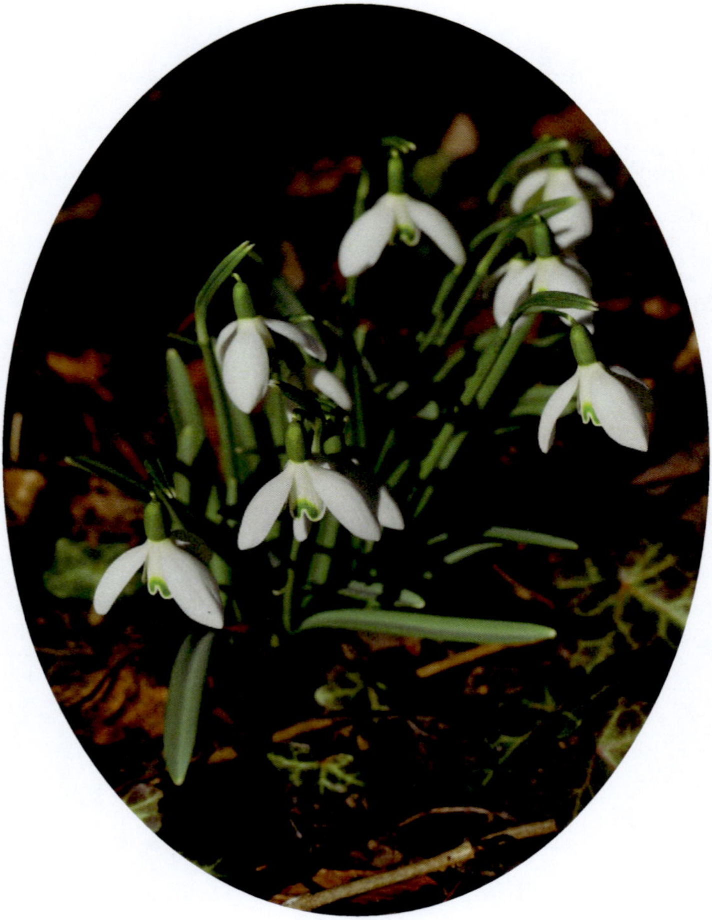

Victoria's Child

We arrived
Heavy with dread
Unable to speak
Victoria's smile was small
Blue eyes sharp
Colourless face
Said she'd just washed her hair
So normal
Seemed grotesque
At this time
'She's in here.'

I stared
Dumbstruck
Little blue dress
Matching boots
Tiny white face
Two-year-old corpse.
I stared
At misshapen nostrils
Dragged by tubes
And desperate attempts
To save her.

I looked at Victoria
Saw dry-eyed purpose
For the funeral test.
I saw her soul
Shrunken with grief
For her dead child.
I found a voice
Embraced her
"God help you." it said
Helplessly
Lovingly.

Worse to come
I will never forget
Her dignity and grace
As she walked up the aisle
Of that church.
Sharp navy coat
Snowdrops
Clutched in white hands
Freshly washed hair
Tumbling glossily
As she went to bury her child.

"All Things Bright and Beautiful"
Rang through choking sobs
Only mistily we see
Bouquets of tiny spring flowers
Around little white coffin.
But undoing came
When Seamus Heaney read
His work for this terrible day:
"Dear girl, why were you born
To cause us all such grief?"
Hearts broke on his words.

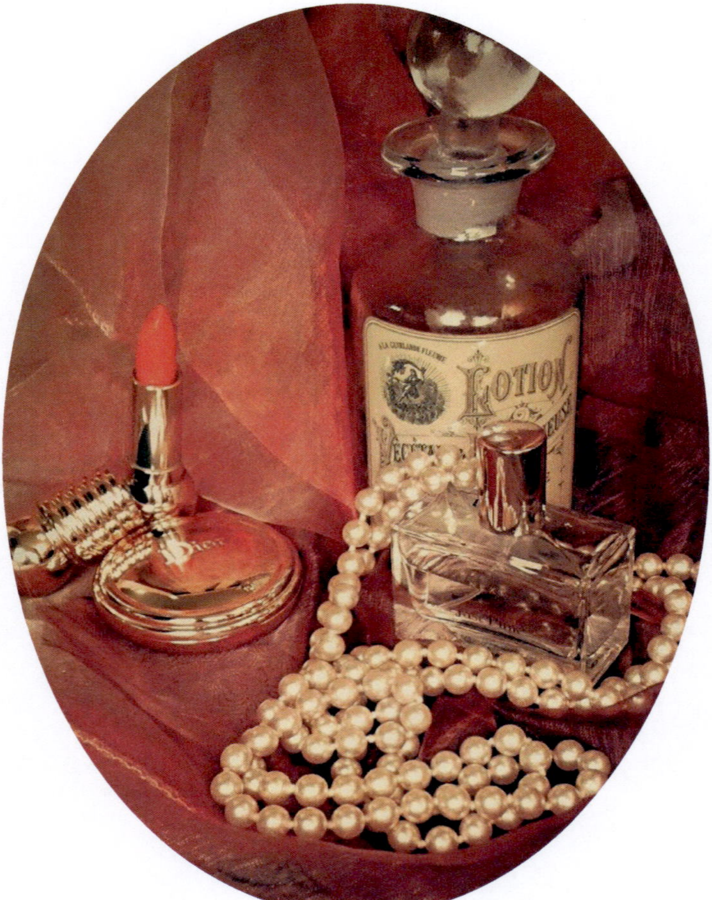
LOTION

The First Chapters

I looked into a mirror on my thirtieth birthday and thought: "How did I survive all that?" But I did and I can still smile, mostly.

Early childhood was a frogspawn and ladybird-collecting odyssey in the fields behind our house, which culminated one day in the unspeakable delight of finding a newt living quietly inside the broken remains of a red plastic telephone. Sadistic impulses were, mercifully, occasional, confining themselves to the systematic de-winging and de-legging of bluebottles, and I would watch with pitiless fascination as the oval black torsos spun helplessly in buzzing agony before being dispatched under my shoe.

Apart from that, I was as hyper-compliant as they came and my later childhood is stiff with memories of family visits to my Aunt Lilian's house, where I would sit obediently, waiting to be spoken to, and doing occasional desultory head counts of the Royal Doulton figurines on the mantelpiece. Even the fire had the wit to behave itself, for not one piece of unruly coal ever fell out of it. The garden was a triumph of ruthless control. A small square of razor-edged grass gave way to bolt upright groups of terrified dahlias, backed by a greenhouse of imprisoned tomato plants. Aunt Lilian's chocolate buns were the only highlight, although I never had the audacity to eat more than two.

Towards adolescence, however, and in the privacy of my bedroom, I experimented with red lipstick and the dubious pleasures of hold-up stockings, female underwear having fallen into that godforsaken chasm between real stockings and tights, and I would sneak to the shop feeling decidedly racy with my newly elongated legs.

Thankfully, the teenage wilderness years were blissfully accommodated by dear Lucy and her family, until, at seventeen, I met Nicolas, a Robert Redford lookalike with a matching IQ. A deep friendship led, unfortunately, to an embittered parting and a blindfolded nosedive for me into the murky depths of bad boys and big motorbikes.

Cheryl lived in the same student house as me at university. Loud, direct and quite ferocious, I instantly hated her, but we got past that, and, as far as alcohol intake went, the early experiments with Lucy turned into the equivalent of serious clinical trials. Cheryl, whose father in America, was a wandering blues pianist, card sharp and alcoholic, had a genetic inheritance of similar capacity, so I, in turn, had an interesting, almost workless final year which culminated in my ambling into what I assumed was the first of my final exams in sociology, only to be confronted by a semi-hysterical young man who informed me that these were the ancient history papers and would I please get out of his seat.

My general quest for meaning and enlightenment took me into nurse training where Kim was waiting, sharp as an alley cat and with high heels to match. By day, we watched bunions being Black-and-Deckered off in theatre and by night, we approached our boyfriend hunts with the same precision.

London beckoned then, with all its confusing mix of the deeply drab and the highly exotic and suddenly, I was thirty.

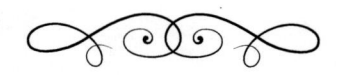

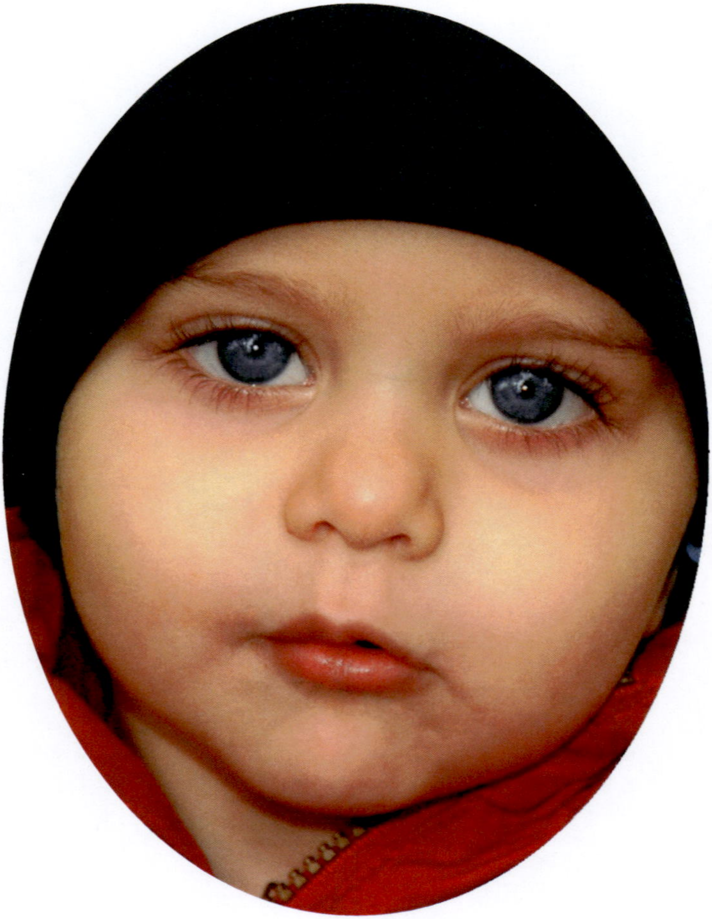

Everyday Love

As I sit here, Lord, before dying embers
I pray that you will listen
To a heartfelt wish
Rising desperately
Amidst contented snores
Within snowbound walls.

Joy was the crystal blue
Of my boy's bright eyes
In the pale early light
When his errant father came.
His cheerful little tree
Bobbing in apology.

Of course, he came in
Of course, I fed him
Of course, I still care.
And he means well
Intends to be different
But I know now, he won't.

He settles in
Stays for a while
Eats his fill
Roasts his feet
While my boy's eyes glow
With desperate love.

But, on Christmas Eve night
His eyes plead
To be released
From our humble fare
And he leaves our bright fire
To stumble through darkness.

He might re-appear
From the cheap delights
Of the crowded pub
Just in time
To start a row
And ruin Christmas.

I know I'm a fool
To hope that he'll change
That one of these years
I won't have to witness
My boy's bitter tears
Of disappointment.

I'll keep the fire burning
I'll bake every day
And I'll watch with great love
As boy becomes man.
But this is the last time
I'll pray for a miracle.

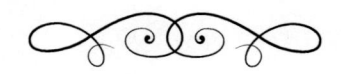

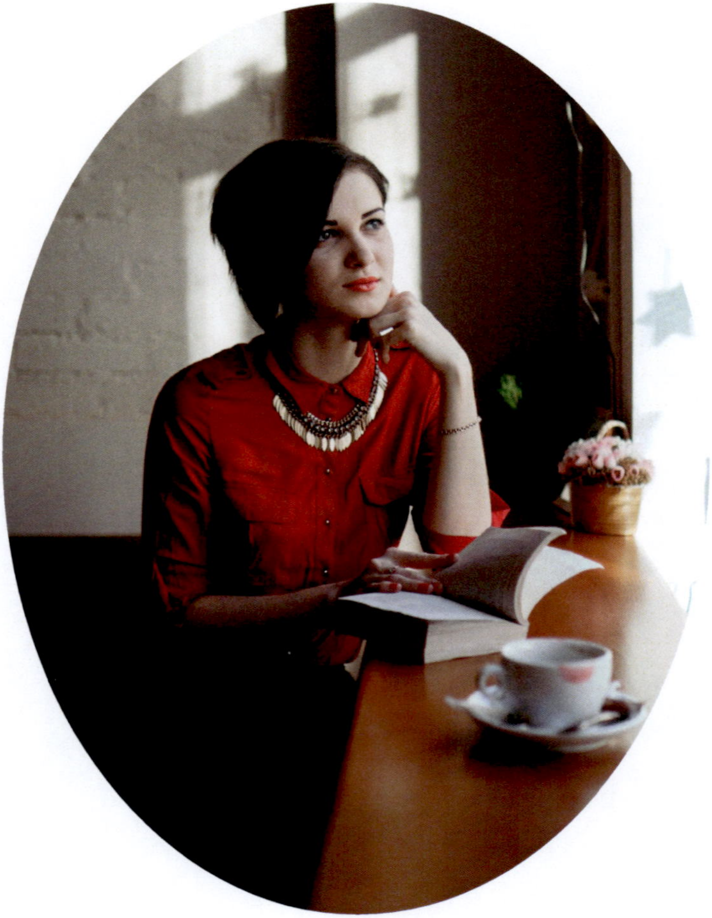

This Life

Complete certainty
Lies only in two places:
That we will die
And that we do not know
How or when.
All else is relative.

But the chances are that we will panic less
And pass more peacefully
When the spectre beckons
If we have lived a life
That we are proud of.

The world owes us nothing
And life is no more
Than mistakes and learning.
We are all alone
However close we are
To others.

The decency of people
And what they think of themselves
Is mostly situational
For none of us know
How we would really be
Until we're tested.

Try throwing us into Auschwitz
For six months
And then look the mirror
And tell me:
Do you still think
You're a really nice person?

So don't be naïve
And lose the idea
That everyone wishes you well.
The more successful you are
The more envy you'll inspire
And envy wants to destroy.

Hold on to your soul
Find out what you believe
Listen to those who love you
Imbue your life with meaning
And one day you'll see
That love is really all that matters.

Listen to Aristotle
And know yourself
As well as you can.
Then don't hang about
Waiting for storms to pass
Learn to dance in the rain.

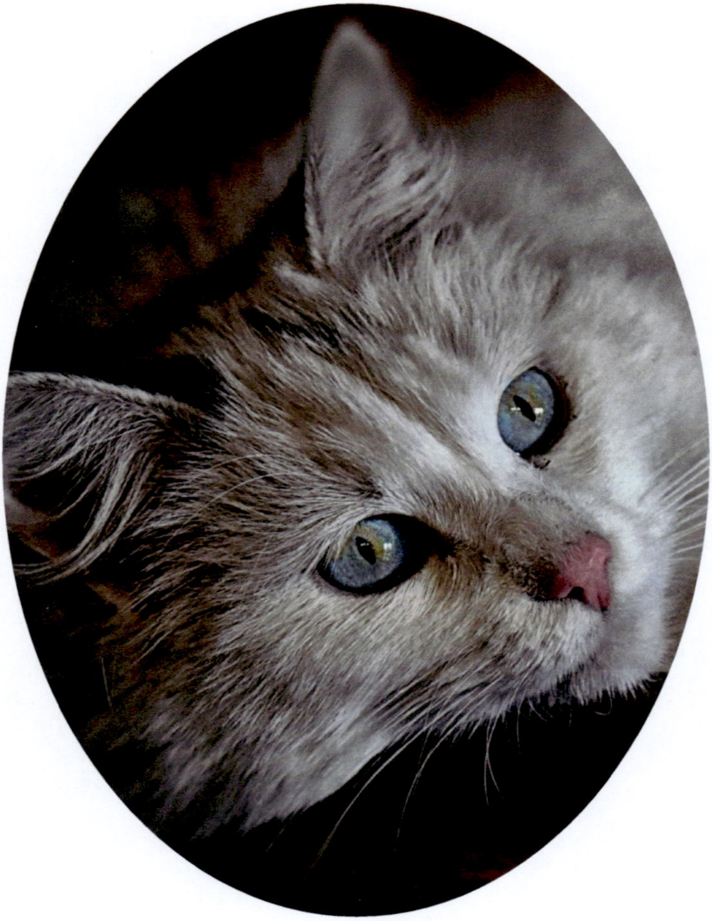

The End of the Road

Max would have been a real man's man, had he not been a cat. From a tiny kitten, he would tolerate only limited cuddling before claws and teeth appeared. 'That's enough of that prissy maternal stuff', he seemed to say. It set up a barrier between us, because I had wanted an affectionate cat. In time, I stopped trying.

Nevertheless, our relationship was mutually respectful. At some point, over his seventeen years, an unspoken agreement was reached: I wouldn't try to make him sit on my lap and he would minimize his propensity to treat me like staff.

He had other qualities, though, that some might admire. Through several house moves, his capacity to find and patrol geographical boundaries, to defend his turf against marauding intruders and to hunt down and kill anything with a pulse that was smaller than himself, made him a formidable force in a garden.

Indoors, Max was a sensualist, especially when an open fire was on offer. He was the biggest cat I've ever seen, and when he wasn't busy keeping a supercilious eye on his human companions or twisting himself into interesting and unlikely contortions, he would stretch from one end of the hearth to the other and, trustingly, go off to sleep like a baby.

Now, though, on the day before Christmas Eve, everything was different. My big tabby was beaten.

A visit, six months ago, to the vet, had removed some of his teeth and confirmed a growing blindness in one eye. His appetite, once voracious, had reduced itself to a delicate series of regular nibbles.
In the last four days, he hadn't eaten at all.

The surgery smelt clean as I carried Max in.
The vet was young, warm and frank.
'You could spend a fortune on tests to find out what's wrong', he said, 'but Max is old and there's a lot that won't improve, no matter what we do. But it's your decision'.

I'm sensible about animals, like my father. He never flogged dead horses. But the speed of my decision startled me 'No', I said, 'I think it's best to let him go'.

It disturbed me somewhat that Max was still walking around the floor. It would have seemed more appropriate if he had been lying, in obvious pain, on the table.

The vet lifted him gently and set him in front of me, as he turned to draw up the injection. There was that endless, awful pause where the only sound was the coarse whirring of the razor as a patch of hair was shaved from Max's leg. I had a sudden, arresting vision of the war-time Jews having their heads shaved, powerless in the face of the Nazis. A bitter taste of something akin to betrayal rose in my throat.

I kissed the little round head as the needle went in. His whole body deflated gently into a most unnatural position, legs splayed out to the sides. I ran my hand over the soft, still warm fur for several seconds. For the first time, I felt no claws against my skin.

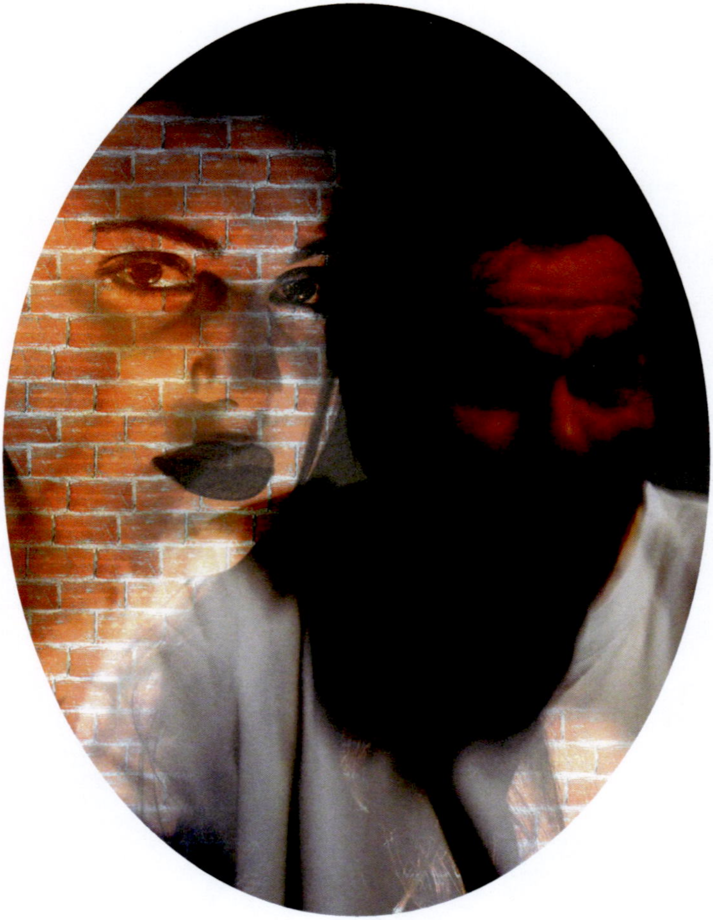

Charade

The urge to interrupt him was overwhelming, but she sat, head bowed, her eyes fixed on the polished toe of his left shoe, her fingers pulling at a piece of skin at the side of one of her nails till it came off, suddenly and painfully, making her gasp, but soundlessly. His flow, thankfully, was uninterrupted. Stella shifted position slightly and pressed her finger tightly to deaden the pain. Lifting her head, she met his eyes for a second and felt as though she would scream if this monstrous farce didn't end soon.

He had the audience enthralled now with his easy wit and confident self-assurance. They just loved their new Victims Commissioner. They knew they'd made the right choice. They knew he was the man for the job. He'd been talking now, without notes, for fifteen minutes, his deep, rich voice rising and falling, reasoning and questioning, hypnotic in its persuasiveness. Anxieties about funding were airbrushed away, fears for the future alleviated. Here, at last, was a man who really, truly cared about people.

Stella glanced around her at the rapt faces. "If only they knew", she thought bitterly. He was winding it all up now, preparing to end on a high note of hope. She retrieved her expensive little bag from under her seat and got ready to leave. He would expect the car to be waiting, warmed up and purring, at the back exit. She hurried out, thunderous applause at her heels, and stepped into the dark, raining coldness outside.

As she knew it would, the engaging smile faded from his lips as he came towards the car and heaved himself in. The usual grim silence between them materialized like a ghost the moment he closed the door. Stella drove quickly through the darkness, her mind racing and her concentration absolute. It was a skill she'd honed over the years, as though she was two separate people. A survival skill. She'd given him no excuse to start anything all day. Everything at home was perfect. But this, she knew, was one of those times when he would do it, just because he could. Nevertheless, he still managed to surprise her.

The big car swept smoothly over the gravel of the drive and slowed to a halt. Stella felt nauseous with anxiety as she stepped out into the darkness. But she didn't even get as far as the front door. Knocked off balance by a blow to the side of her head, she found her face rammed against the harsh pebbledash of the front wall of her home, while blows rained into her back, making her crumple to the ground.

"You can sleep in the car tonight," he growled into her ear as he pulled her keys from her hand. "Fucking bitch. You couldn't even manage a round of applause".

Stella heard the sound of his mobile suddenly and the smile in his voice as he spoke into it. His grip on her hair tightened, pulling mercilessly at the roots and forcing her face into the wet mud of a bay tree container.

'Thank you so much', he purred, 'Wonderful evening. Just home. Everything's perfectly under control now.'

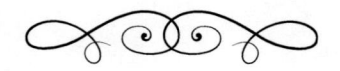

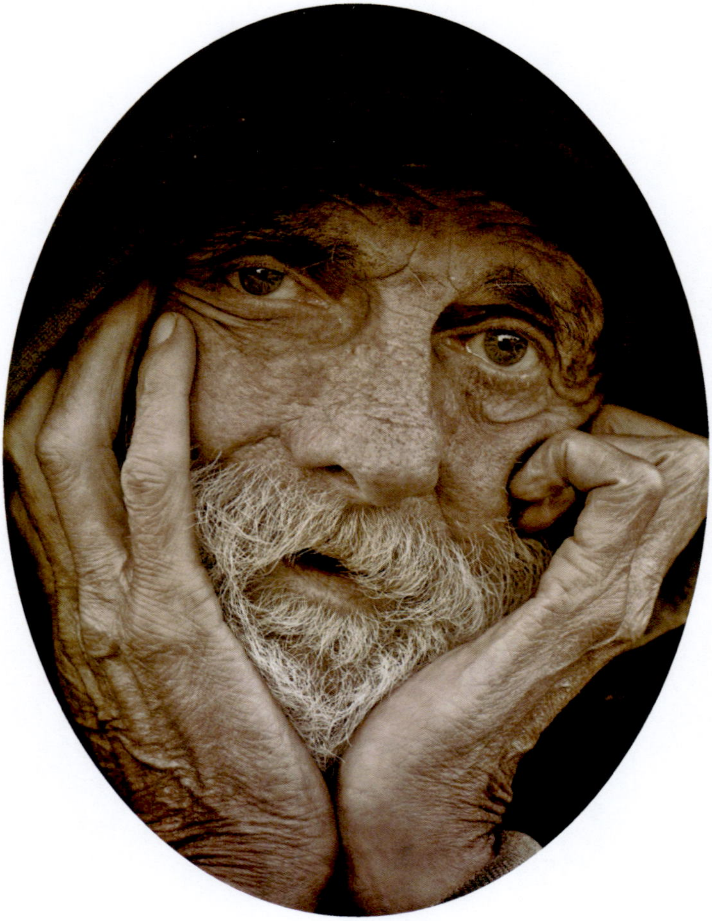

Haiku

White flakes on green leaves
Melt to water in sunrays
Fall back into earth

Woman loves her child
Loves with feral claws of steel
And the lightest touch

In ancient armchair
Old man sleeps by glowing fire
Death creeps, waits, triumphs

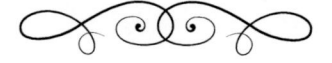

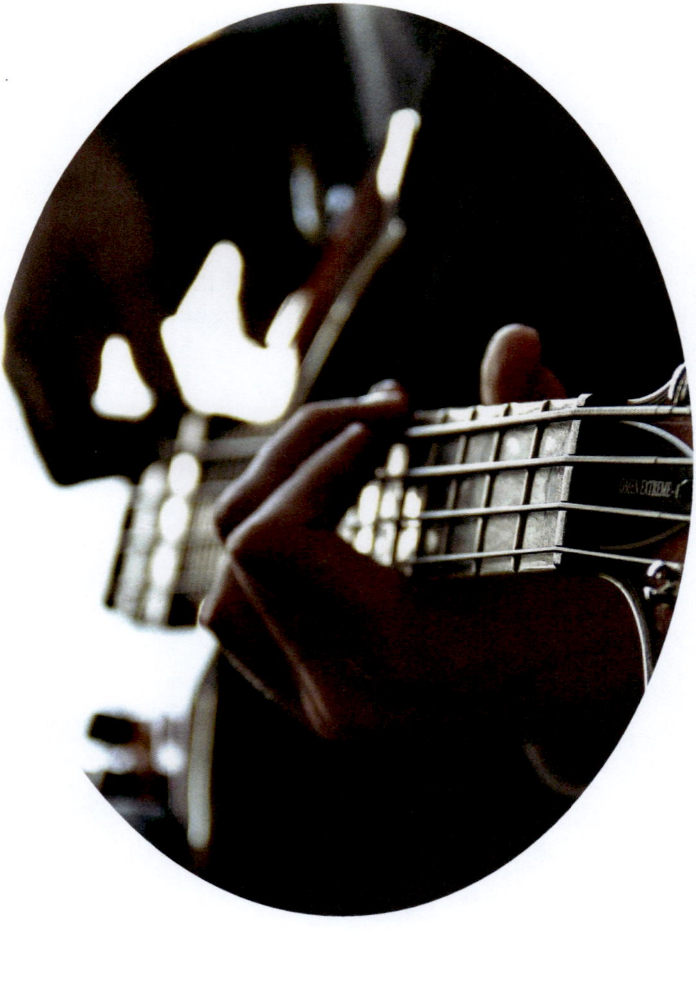

Ending

I left my lover on his birthday
Deliberately
To cause maximum pain.
'You've no heart', he said.
'I know', I said.
'You broke it'.

We were not young
When we crashed
Together
The house we built
Was the child
We would never have.

Ten years it took me
To know you
To know what you really were
To move from breathless closeness
Through shock and disappointment
To this bitter place.

You heard your music
You heard your own voice
I listened to all of you
Because I loved you.
But too late I realised
You did not hear me.

Music is your true mistress
Your real and only love
Capricious and demanding
She beguiles you
And you fall at her feet
In endless worship.

But I won't be your sideshow
Or your little kitchen maid
I cannot compete
With your Goddess
I deserve better
I deserve to be heard

The end came
Our hate
As intimate
As our love
Unable to agree
On the colour of the sky
On a cloudless day.

So shout with your loud guitar
Seduce with your pretty notes
And your shy smile
Let them believe
There is no darkness
For your show must go on.

And how do I continue
In this unwelcome, bitter space
That I call a life?
I mourn
I exist
Until I live
Once more.

You're a memory now
A sealed wound
An occasional dream
Of sea-green eyes.
I walk carefully now
With a quiet joy
But the music
Forever
Is bittersweet.

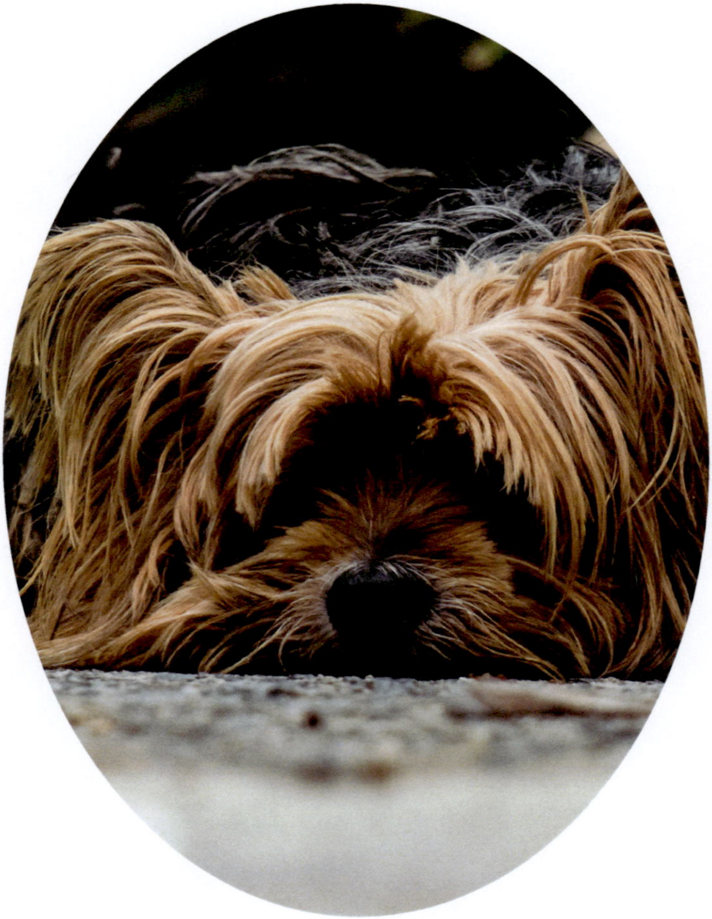

Letting Go

In the time that Anne had owned her, Molly had never been a particularly healthy dog. Battered and abandoned as a puppy, she had endured a lifetime of being unable to walk, but had been, somehow, rescued, until her new owner's health had collapsed, at which point Anne, my colleague, had offered her a home.

For the next seven years, the level of loving attention lavished upon this creature would have inspired envy in many a child, and she was spoken of as though she was the only dog in the world.

Anne had had a hard life. One of a family of ten, her father had been an abusive drunk who had terrorized his wife and family. An exceptionally pretty girl, Anne had worked hard all her life, but had had an accidental daughter at sixteen and had been forced by her parents to give her up for adoption. Marrying in her twenties, she had been abandoned by her husband, leaving her with two small children, one of whom later died of leukaemia.

Occasionally, she would talk about this little boy, and how she had gone almost mad with grief, ranting and pleading with the Almighty in the forsaken hours before dawn, before the terrible, anguished, final scene as he slipped quietly away from her. Tears would still well in her blue eyes as she spoke, almost forty years later.

Molly's health, never robust, gradually deteriorated over the space of two years. Regular and seemingly endless, visits to the vet, produced a series of diagnoses, chief amongst which was cancer, but also included blindness and finally, canine dementia. Nevertheless, Molly continued to eat and drink and did not appear to be in pain.

Meanwhile, things in Anne's household took a turn for the bizarre. A pram appeared, complete with pillow and duvet. This was followed, several weeks later, by a coffin, its insides lined with an offensively loud pink satin, and its lid inscribed with its future occupant's name.

I happened to be visiting one day and took a peek inside the pram. I'm not sure what I expected, but it wasn't what I saw. 'Isn't she looking so much better?' crooned Anne, lifting the duvet gently for me to see. My pity and distaste must have been clearly visible behind my polite and humourless smile. The animal was barely recognisable as a dog. Huge, unsightly lumps protruded across its body, the white skin strained and balding as it struggled to contain them. One pathetic little tooth hung crookedly from its top lip and its eyes, hooded and unseeing, darted in confusion at being disturbed.

Time dragged on with news of further deterioration over several weeks. Even Anne knew, eventually, that the game was up. But still, she didn't act.
I was getting angry now, at the imagined suffering.
But Anne was, somehow, inaccessible.
Normally so open, she had ring-fenced herself and her dog into a private space, all support spurned.

'I'll do it myself, in my own time', was all she'd say.
Eventually, she did. Quietly, reverently and alone, she went to the vet for the last time and saw Molly off on her last journey.

I saw her shortly afterwards and enquired how she was.

'I feel really calm', she said, 'for the first time in years.'
I raised an eyebrow.

'I got to choose, you see', she smiled, 'I had her for seven years and I chose when to let her go.'
I nodded, understanding at last.
Her son had been seven years old when he had died.

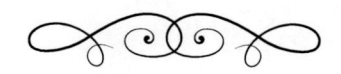

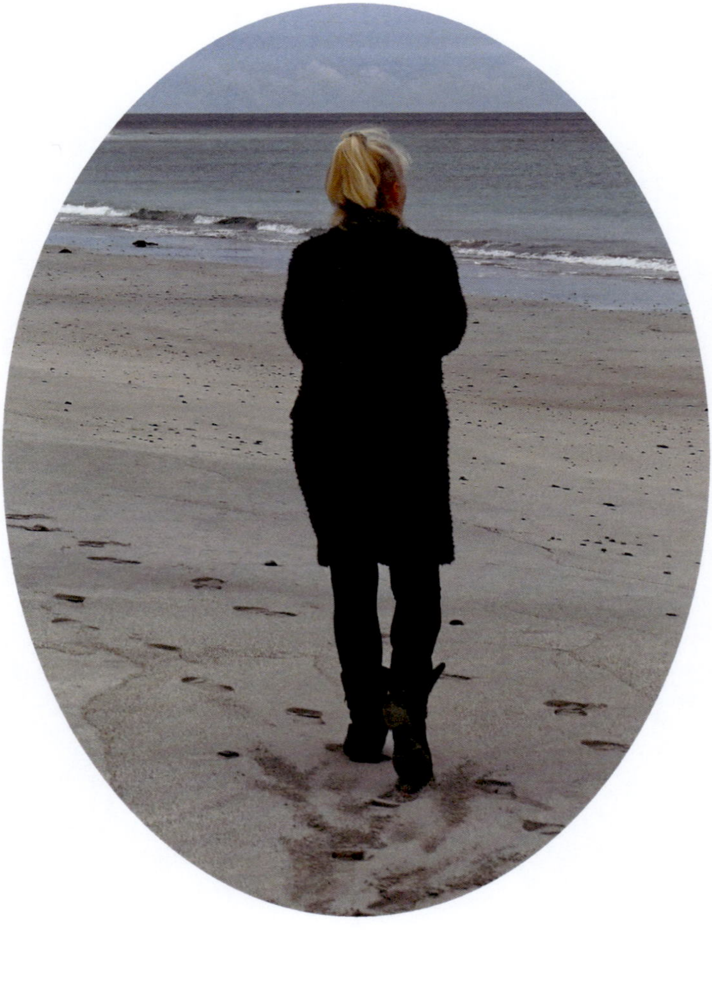

The Parting of the Veils

Something interesting happened to me around the age of fifty-five. It wasn't an event; more the beginning of a process which still continues. To describe it is to liken it to the gradual lifting of a series of veils or illusions which had coloured my thoughts and perceptions for many years, sometimes seeming to enable me, but at others, preventing clarity that was needed.

It all began with the unwelcome realisation that, whether I liked it or not, my youth was gone. I was in the autumn of my life and my mind and body bore witness to its events in scars and attitudes. A level of wisdom had been hard won and with it came a measure of contentment, but a certain wistful sadness lurked in its corners, for it's unlikely that I would ever allow myself the same reckless spontaneity of youth.

So never again will I run with complete abandon through the streets of Paris at midnight with people I barely know, or sleep fitfully on the floors of European train stations. Never again will I work till 3am in a Japanese nightclub and be back on duty as a nurse at eight in the morning, or shelter a diamond dealer from gangsters in Marseilles (the large sapphire in payment seemed well worth it at the time though). I probably won't ever experience the craziness and fun of managing a rock band again and I definitely won't embark on a three-day train journey from Belfast to southern Spain, whether I think I'm in love or not.

I know all sorts of things that eluded me for years. I know about the illusions that advertisers create: how hanging almost anything on a beautiful woman will sell it and that looking at too much of it can make a pretty woman feel ugly. I know that human nature can be a weak and contemptible thing and that not every friendship lasts. I know, too, that passion is a kind of madness and the worst possible basis upon which to make long-term decisions, yet we all do it. Most of all, I know that time is too precious to waste on pointless moping about poor choices in the past. Health, strength, love, kindness and good friends are what matter.

I'm not too old for most things, if truth be told. Shopping and cocktails on a Saturday afternoon is a glorious addiction, as is pottering around markets, hotdog in one hand and battered basket in the other. And of course, if I really wanted to, there's nothing to stop me popping over to London for afternoon tea at the Ritz. Nowadays though, I'd probably pass on the potential liaison with the good-looking Mafiosi type at the bar.

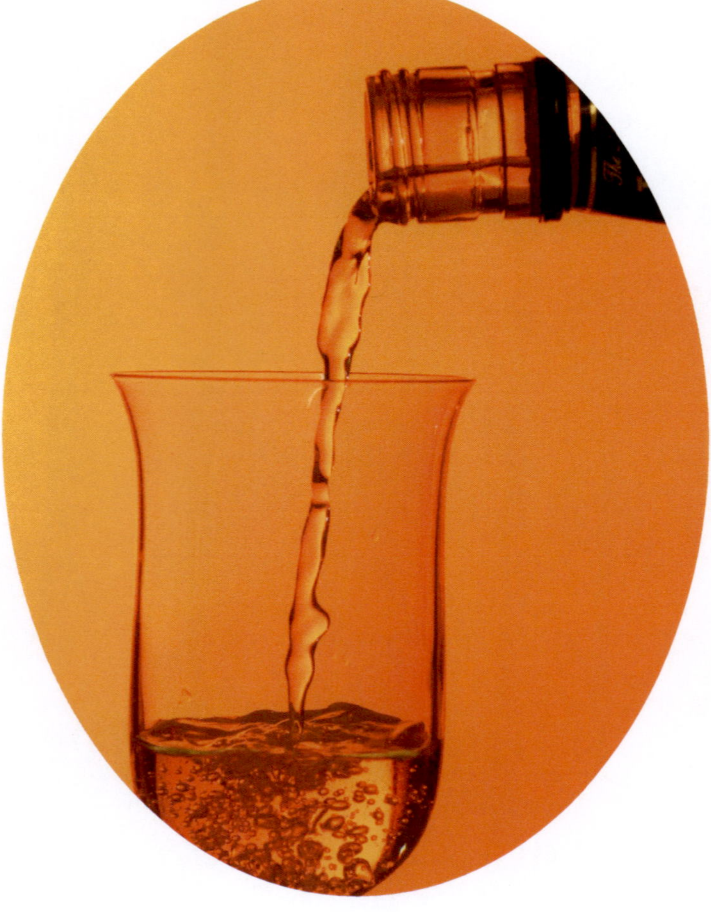

Fallout

It was almost four o'clock. The Saturday afternoon crowd was building as Joe entered the darkened bar. With practised deftness, he moved towards the back, the holdall held casually at his side.

At 4:30, the Aberdelgy Arms pasted its contents, atrociously, onto the pavement and hurled itself into history as an unspeakable obscenity.

'Well done, lad. Six Brits. Good job.' The commander didn't mention the other nine deaths. Joe accepted the proffered glass and the warm backslap. The whiskey felt cool and crisp in his mouth. He began to relax.

Almost forty years later, Joe switched the TV off, yawned and began to prepare for bed. He was fairly contented these days, but yet another programme about victims had irritated him tonight.

'It'd been a war, for Chrissake. What did they expect?' he thought angrily, as he put his whiskey bottle away.

The sudden screeching to a halt of car brakes outside startled him. He headed for the window as the car took off again, screaming into the darkness.

'Bloody joyriders', he thought grumpily.

Joe stared hard. Half-hidden behind the one bush in his garden was the unmistakeable figure of a boy. Amazed, Joe opened the door.

'You OK, son?' he called warily.

The boy, no more than fourteen, jumped up, his forehead bleeding from a gash.

'I don't know where I am', he blurted out. 'I don't know this place.'

Joe sighed. He didn't need this at one in the morning.

'Where are you from?' he asked softly.

'East Belfast. Glenwell Children's Home.'

'Well', said Joe, 'you'd better come in. I'll get you a taxi.'

The boy sat uneasily at the kitchen table, his long adolescent fingers gripping a mug of tea while Joe dabbed at the cut with pieces of wet kitchen roll.

'How come you're so far from home?' asked Joe.

'They threw me out of the car. I was scared. I never done it before. I hit my head on the ground.'

'Bastards', thought Joe, applying a plaster.

'How come you live in Glenwell?' he asked.

The boy stiffened slightly, his blue eyes filling with pain. Pity rose heavily in Joe.

'My Ma died of an overdose and my Da's a nutter.' He hesitated momentarily and then continued:

'He said they were really happy till my Granda died in the troubles. My Granny went mad after it and they were all sent to foster homes. My Da ended up selling drugs. That's when he met my Ma.'

The taxi's horn blared outside. Joe pressed twenty pounds into the boy's hand.

'Thanks mate', he said, with an unexpected, winning little smile. 'Here.' He handed a keyring to Joe, a little grinning leprechaun dangling from it.

'How did your Granda die?' asked Joe suddenly.

'A bomb. A place called the Aberdelgy Arms.'

Joe was still awake at six am, the whiskey bottle empty beside him. He rose, stumbling with drink. The leprechaun grinned mercilessly from the mantelpiece. It was one of those occasional nights when he wished he had been caught.

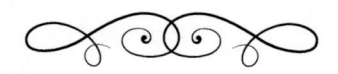

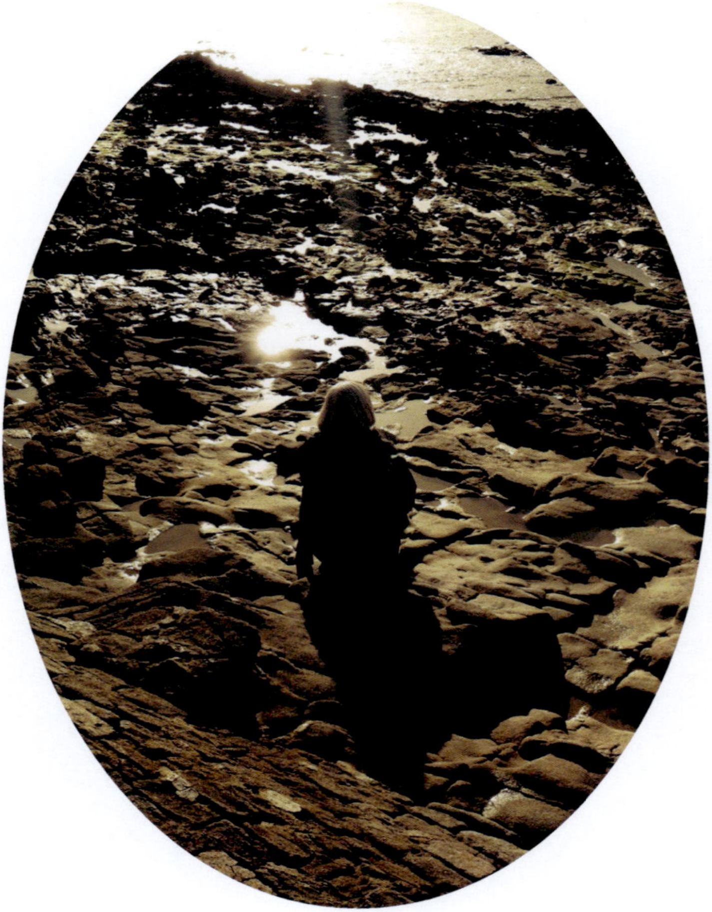

Loss

2012
Reality Year
When veils
Shifted, shimmered
And finally lifted.
The ugly truth
Cornered at last
Sat crouching
Gaping
Waiting for me
To embrace it.

I don't want to approach you
Vile, wretched creature.
Don't want to hear
What you try to tell me.
I prefer my veils
With their colours and slants
And justifications
Of self and others.

Don't want to know that I've lost everything
For a second time.
Don't want to know
That I've wasted
Totally
The last ten years of my life.
Don't want to think
That I'm pining for a house

That I never loved when I lived in it.
But do love now
When it's aged a little
And looks welcoming and gentle.

Don't want to think
That I'll be eaten alive
With envy for someone
Whose career is finally taking off
After we split.
Who, by virtue of doing what he loves
Is in a position of constant opportunity
To find someone new
While I work every weekend
Because there's nothing else to do.

Don't want to acknowledge hating my job
For thirty years
And not getting out.
Don't want to see
That my circle of close friends
Is reduced
To maybe four
If I'm lucky.
Don't want to feel
This pain of neglect
Of selfish lack of care
From those who shouted loudest
About loyalty.

Don't want to face
The grim and lonely reality
That I'm nearly sixty
Hair is grey
Body is ruined

And there's no spark
No joy.
That I've despaired
And no one came
That I'm alone in the dark.
That some days
All I want
Is to sit crouching
In a black shawl
Staring into embers
Never emerging.

Truth sits
Seeming to smirk
Waiting for the fool
To reach out
Through the veils
And fold it into a bitter embrace.
But as she approaches
And finds courage
To sit down beside it
She sees
Not a smirk, nor a jeer
But a sad little creature
Harmless, lonely
Worthy of love
Worthy of her love.
She picks it up gently
Cradling it
And weeping, compassionate
She carries it away.

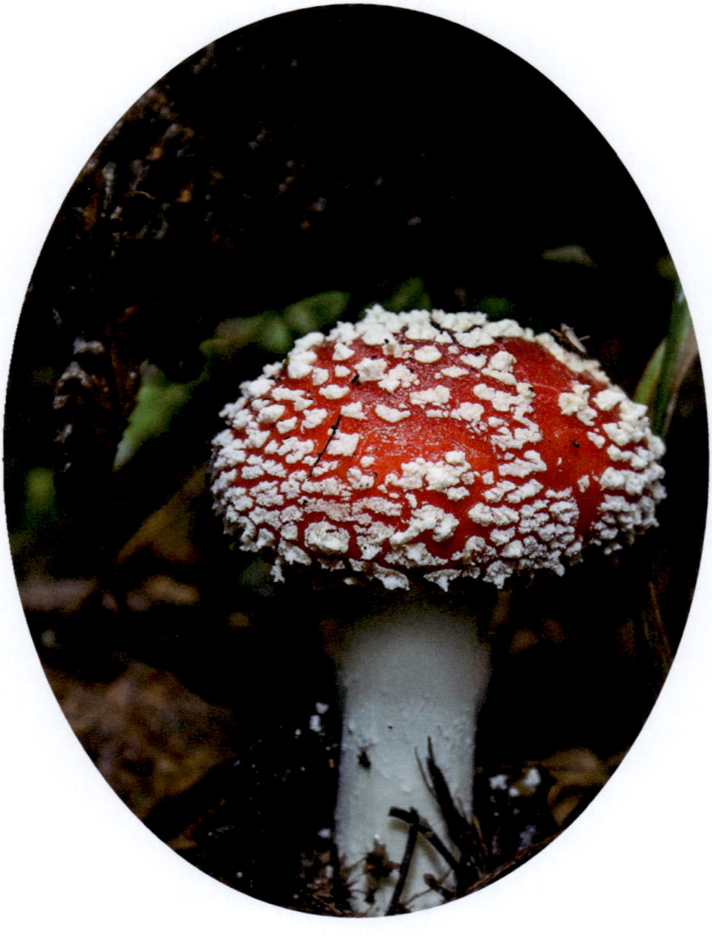

Autumn

Pink dawn seeps
Through lace curtains of white mist
To a low slung, heatless sun
In a bald, blue expanse.
Fingers of startling light
Poke through laden branches
Of myriad colour
And berried glory.

Earth leaks
Brown smells.
Sprouting monstrous pagan armies
Of unwholesome fungi
While black things gorge
On the fruited detritus
Of summer.

Rich, brazen colours
Of final flowers
Stand in open defiance
Of winter's death knell.
While branches labour to support
Voluptuous clumps
Of ripened, seductive fruit
Begging to be devoured.

Down the long ages
Man and woman gather in.
Barns and cellars bulging
With nature's offerings.
It is a beautiful thing
This harvest
This glorious excess
Before the deluge comes.

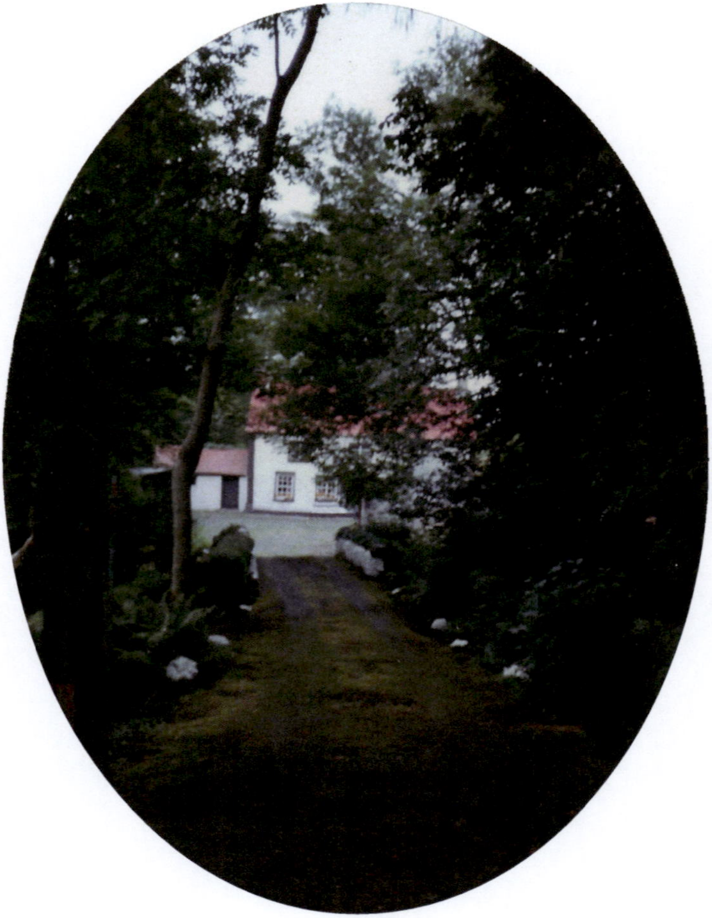

Searching for Home

The car is warm, verging on discomfort. Outside, the day is perfect. I let the breeze in to fan my face as I drive between extremes. I've left the sullen detritus of the estate, with its empty crisp packets and small herds of children on bikes in barren spaces and now I'm cruising through suburban leafiness, past elegant dwellings set back from the road amid manicured lawns and carefully sculpted mounds of tasteful shrubs. The countryside beckons and embraces my quickening car.

White bungalow blight is everywhere. Square, basic boxes dumped charmlessly in the middle of fields without so much as a tree to soften the visual offense of the bland, harsh lines. It's a depressing disease of the 1960s when people began to take Spanish holidays and returned to build villas with entertainingly elongated pitched roofs and outdoor balconies. Like any disease worth its salt, these early specimens mutated into a more resistant local strain, losing the mock-Spanish effect and hardening into the rectangular white boxes that dot the countryside with alarming regularity. Thankfully, it's been curtailed somewhat by an injection of imagination and creativity in recent years, for nowadays, there are some truly lovely houses peeping out from behind clumps of willow and conifer, their beauty no more than a delightful hint as I whizz past their gates.

Yet the truth is that I'm not looking for anything like that. Neither am I looking for the utilitarian farmhouses with their pebble-dashed walls enclosing freezing and unused sitting rooms stuffed to capacity with heavy, dark furniture and generations of hysterically ugly heirlooms.

No, what I want is simple and authentic and I think I'll know it when I find it. It's a fantasy, really, but it exists somewhere in reality. I'll describe it to you as I drive along, for it's probably down a pretty little side-road like the one I'm turning into now and it's little more than an old stone-built cottage.

The front garden is a glorious riot of hollyhocks, delphiniums, foxgloves and roses, extending round the corner to become a kitchen garden of herbs, fruit and home-grown vegetables.

'Come in', I'll say to you and you'll step onto a flagstone floor and into a sizeable space which you'll recognise as the kitchen and living room all in one. There'll be a cheery open fire in a large stone fireplace with an old clock ticking reassuringly above it and an ancient Labrador stretched before it. Comfortable chairs will surround this focal point and you'll know immediately that you can make yourself at home.

A large wooden table is off to one side and a big rustic jug of wild flowers adorns it. There's a cheerful mismatch of bright china on the Welsh dresser behind it and you might have to chase an occasional hen from underneath the table.

The sun slants warmly through the top of the open stable-type door at the back and you'll be offered tea and home-baked cake when you arrive. If you're staying overnight after a jovial meal and plenty of wine, you'll sleep in a luxuriously comfortable bed with feather pillows and the quiet scent of lavender all around.

The next morning, if the weather is fine, you'll step outside to the ancient enclosed courtyard for breakfast and you might be surprised at how many inhabitants greet you. As you sit in a comfortable wicker chair sipping your tea and eating your toast, you could find yourself nudged by a curious horse or two, for they like their treats and they've wandered from the paddock to greet you. A number of cats will observe quizzically from their perches on the nearby cobbles and if you're lucky you may even get a morning parade of ducklings on their way to the pond.

After breakfast, you can root around in the hayshed and collect the night's eggs from the speckled hens, and when you leave, the boot of your car will bulge with home-grown vegetables, jams and freshly baked bread.

I hope you've enjoyed your time in this homely little place. You may even have made a new friend or two, for the neighbours

often call. One way or another, you'll have been welcomed warmly and you'll know you can call again whenever you want.
No phone call required.

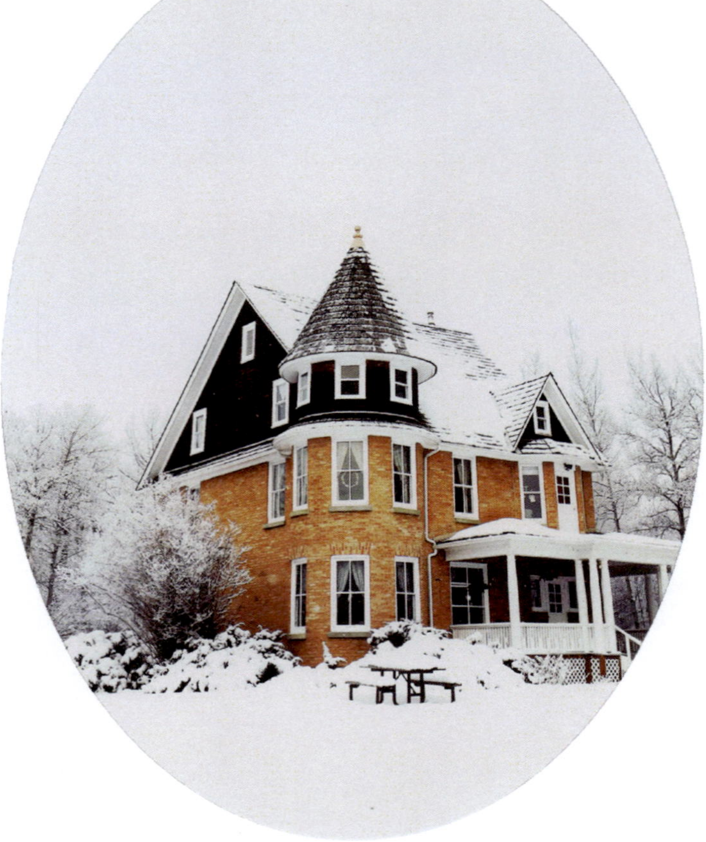

Home

Lucy is and always has been, my best friend. When I was eleven and just starting in a new, seemingly huge school, home consisted of an ill, withdrawn father, a hard-working, no-nonsense mother, a terminally angry younger sister and myself, whose major skill appeared to lie in elevating a posture of feigned indifference to the level of an art form.

Tired of dodging the bullets, I actively sought out the company of this skinny, retiring creature from the country whose capacity for listening quietly far outstripped my own. But Lucy was not the blank slate that she claimed. She was fearless in the ways of the countryside and she knew things that I didn't. I listened, horrified, as she explained how sex worked; I accepted my first cigarette from her and my first taste of surreptitious alcohol from a stubby quarter bottle of vodka concealed in the bushes.

To this day, I don't think she fully appreciated what it meant to me to be able to simply hang out at the weekends, to be accepted and not criticised by her family, from her deeply kind, if slightly mad, mother to her generally silent father, whose eyes harboured a deep twinkle and whose ability to speak volumes rested on a remarkable ability to arch one eyebrow, the height of which depended on the content of what he was listening to. Lucy's elder sister was as odd as mine. She joined in almost nothing with the rest of us and would sit hunched and glowering, in front of the fire, sporting her father's socks and slippers. Her brother was a replica of his father, except he smiled more and her younger sister, Liza, was a pretty, leggy, doe-eyed charmer who, today, is as eccentric as her mother ever was.

The first time I visited, the whole place was a wonderland of deep snow. The large red brick house in its own rambling grounds and surrounded by out-buildings, sat at the end of an untidy, green-gated drive. To the right was a small, ice-covered lake with a watermill and we spent much of that afternoon on a rowing boat in the middle of it, carving our way through the ice for fun. Dinner was bacon, turnip and potatoes and after that I never looked back. From eleven to seventeen, my weekends were spent there, whether it was three of us, huddled and laughing, in a double bed with one hot water bottle against the freezing cold of the upstairs rooms, or walking along the nearby railway line at twilight, telling secrets and dodging the bats on warm nights.

We walked miles beside Liza's horse on country roads in the heat, taking turns to ride and we helped to serve dinner in newly cut hayfields, the men descending, red-faced and sweating, to eat hot food at midday in the middle of summer. Those teenage memories sit, to this day, like little treasures in my mind, easily accessed and warming to the soul, like home.

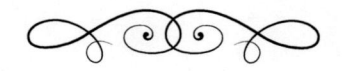

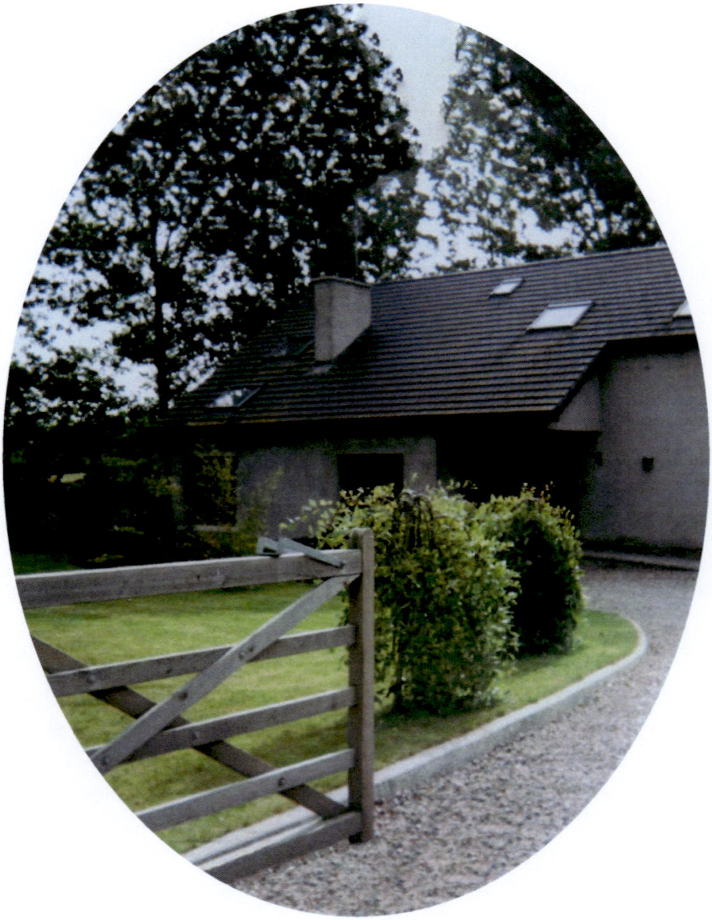

Portmore

Here you are
Shabby now
But magnificent
Unpolished in nine months
Cobwebs in corners
Moss on your roof
Weeds in the drive
You're less snappy and sharp now
Less arrogant.
But so much more human
So much more beautiful
I want to take care of you
To show you my love.
Too late.

God help you, poor thing
Never stood a chance
Weren't loved properly
When you were born
Out of the ground.
You seemed too big
Too much
Too full of struggle
For your parents.
And they hadn't the wit
To give you time
To wait
While you matured
To your present glory.

Your childhood could have been better
Different, joyful
Filled with children sounds
Loving your space.
But they weren't welcome
Were pushed away
And didn't come.
So you never became
The warm family home
You were meant to be.

And now you sit here
Secluded
Surrounded by trees
Tall, evergreen, protective
In your little corner.
Gardens high-summer ripe
Raspberries blushing, unpicked
Greenhouse empty.
I walk around
Sadly
Smelling the rosemary
On fingertips
Trailing hands on purple lavender
Marvelling at the size
Of the fatsia plant
Heartbroken.

Our summerhouse will never exist
Over there among the rowan trees
Or the vegetable garden
Beside the pergola.
I'll never rise early
To search the lawn

For mysterious toadstools
That emerge in the night
Damp and magical.
I'll never bake cakes
Make afternoon tea
Or serve it
On bright blue and white china
In the secret garden
In sunshine
Among blue geraniums
And giant hostas.

Gone too are the old wicker chairs
And crackling warmth
Of the chimenea
Till one in the morning
When we made toast
And ate it
Fresh from the embers
Memory drifts
Into apples, pears, plums, greengages
From Kathy's garden
And our laughing attempts
To press our own juice
In the autumn
When leaves
Were thousandfold
And air was clear
And sharp as a blade.

Parties are over
Candles snuffed
Only stillness
Of trees against moon.

No more
Will we crowd round singers
No more
Will voices rise together
No more
Will the sweet notes
Of the beautiful fool
Dance languidly over the top.
And how you came into your own
At Christmas.
Gloried in your decorations
Opened your doors
To all and sundry
Yelled: 'Come in! Come in!'
Come see my three Christmas trees
Come and admire my candles, my ivy.
Eat from my table
Let me fill you with warmth and colour
And embrace you with love.'

Sadness now
Wreathes you
Like mist
And whispers
Like ghosts of children
In your empty rooms.
You're lonely
Away down here
With your 'For Sale' sign
Forlorn, at the gate.
You're barely cared for
And yet, still so young.
I'm sitting here
Among trailing ferns.

And you're hushed
Awaiting your fate
Helpless in the face of it.
I breathe your beauty into me.
I love you now
And I wish
You'd never been born.

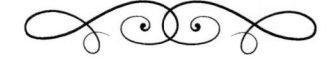

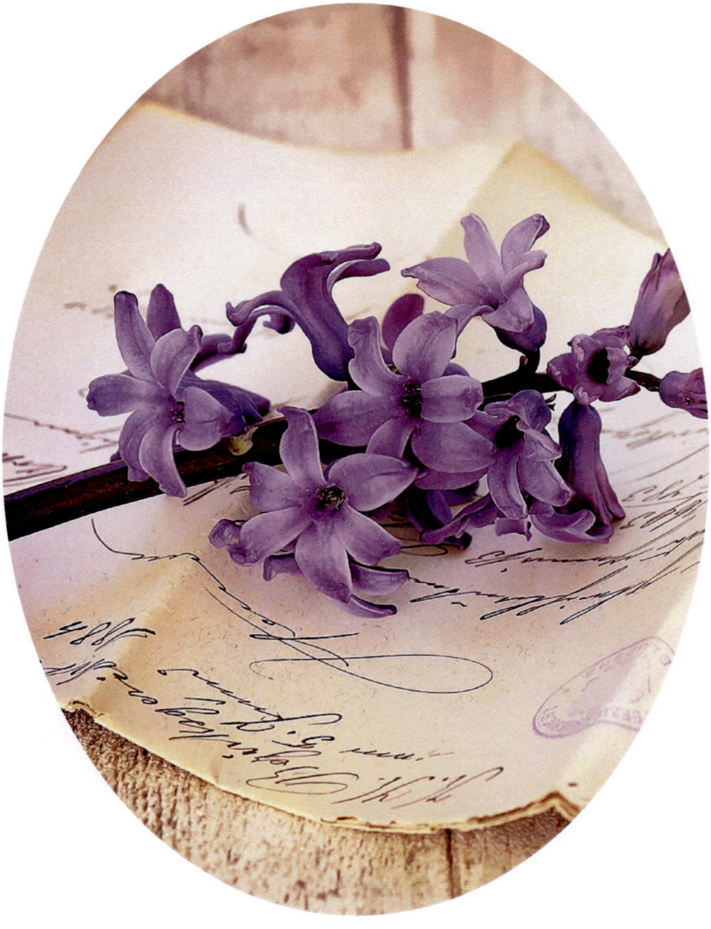

Frozen in Time

The scent of violets hung thickly in the bedroom.
Lauren rammed the stopper into the bottle of purple perfume and opened the window. It was still snowing. A thin stream of icy air threaded in.
    'It'll keep the body cool', she thought dispassionately.
Her mother's lifeless face, framed by prematurely grey hair and carven now, like marble, was still as glacially beautiful as ever.
Bitterly, Lauren remembered her own decision, at ten, to abandon forever her fruitless attempts to make contact with this remote, colourless woman with the dead eyes.
    Carefully, she opened the drawer of the bedside cabinet and lifted out the old leather case. With a strong sense of the forbidden at her heels, she hurried downstairs and turned its enticing little key. Her father would soon be back from the undertaker's. Lauren stared at the few, aged contents: a tiny perfume bottle, a compass and a letter, which she began to read:
July 1944
My darling Isabella,
I'm sure you won't receive this, but I must write to say good-bye. I'm alone in some Godforsaken field in France. It's snowing and I've lost my compass, so I'm stuck. The Germans are very near.
    You've made me so happy, my love. Remember Paris? Remember how you danced in your wonderful red dress?
And how we laughed in that little café? Such precious memories! Take care, darling, and always wear the violet perfume for me.
    Yours forever,
    Laurence.
Lauren's mind reeled. She was born in 1945. It was now 1963 and she was eighteen. Yet her parents said they had met after the war. That had to be after 1945.
    Her father's kindly face appeared, suddenly, at the door, concern etched across his features at her distraught expression.

Wordlessly, she thrust the case towards him. To her surprise, he simply sat down heavily and turned to her.

'You should've known this years ago', he began, 'but your mother would never let me tell you. Laurence was her lover. They met in Paris, in 1943, and he died in that field. Your mother had taken the compass from his pocket, just to look at it, and had forgotten to replace it before he left. She never forgave herself. He was the love of her life. In fact, she was pregnant with you when he died. I met her in 1946 when you were a baby and I fell in love instantly. She was so beautiful and sad. So fragile.' He paused, remembering. 'She never loved me, but she married me anyway. I didn't realise that I'd never melt her heart. She was always his, right to the end. I'm so sorry, love. I'm not your dad, biologically anyway. But I've always loved you so very, very much. I hope you know that.'

Lauren sat silently, gazing into the lively fire. Then she glanced at him, seeing fear in his eyes for the first time in her life. Impulsively, she took his hand and slid onto the floor at his feet.

'I do know it', she said quietly, 'You're the only real dad I've ever known.'

He hugged her tightly. 'Here, love. I brought you these', he said softly, handing her a small bunch of early daffodils. She smiled and glanced outside. It had stopped snowing at last.

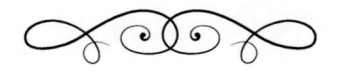

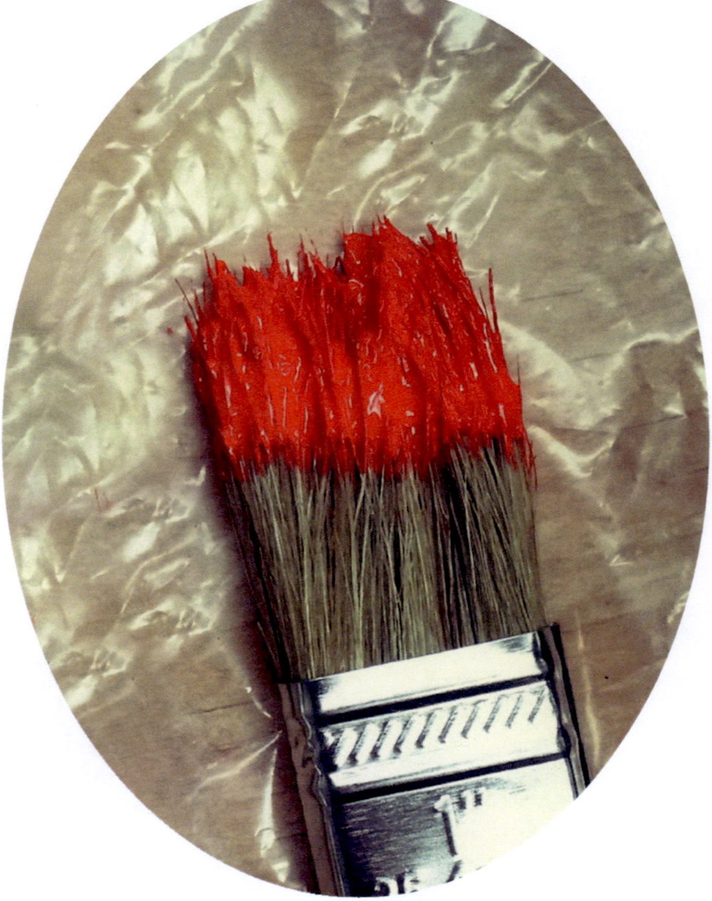

Acts of Love

Carefully, Sean placed the lid onto the tin of paint and stood back to admire his handiwork. The front door gleamed redly back at him as his son's little head suddenly popped into view from the hallway.

"Your hands are all red, daddy," he announced. "It's like blood."

"I know, son," Sean replied. "but it's only paint."

Sean could see the slight figure of his wife, Maeve, approaching form shopping. She smiled her approval at him as she reached the door.

"Thanks, love," she said softly. "Connor's got his red front door for Christmas at last."

Sean gazed at her trusting, open face and felt his heart swelling with love for this sweet woman who had transformed his attitude to life in the past few years and had given him the unbelievable gift of a son. Instinctively, he reached out to stroke her hair, but she dodged away, laughing.

"Not with those hands!" she said, disappearing indoors.

Left alone, Sean's mind turned again to the forthcoming afternoon. Not for the first time, a wave of nausea overcame him. All he could focus on were the hard, grey beads of Casey's eyes and the affable, even-toned menace in his voice.

"I know things have changed for you, Sean," he'd said, "but we need one last thing from you. Those alibis we provided for the two murders are worth a lot. You owe us, Sean."

"What do you want me to do?" Sean had said flatly.

"There's a place beside the shopping centre. I want you to put a device in it. You'll be collected from home at two on Saturday and driven there. After that…" Casey had shrugged, "you're free."

Sean knew he had no real choice. The real IRA were a harsh bunch. But he didn't want to do this anymore. He had a life beyond the cause. Maeve's voice interrupted his thoughts.

"We'll be leaving for mum's around two, Sean. If we go straight there, we'll be in Newry by three."

Two hours later, Sean was picking his way impatiently through a number of elderly people towards the dim interior of the little shop which claimed to sell just about everything. Tom Baird's shop wasn't a place for the wealthy. Small coins changed from one aged hand to another. The frail, bespectacled owner smiled at him as he passed with the black holdall, which he placed quickly under a shelf crammed with nails and plugs at knockdown prices.

Moments later, Sean was back in the car, heading quickly out of town. Tom Baird's soft, unassuming features danced sickeningly before his eyes. A delicate, silvery sound tinkled suddenly and unexpectedly from his mobile, announcing a text. Automatically, he began to read:

"No white spirit left, so we've stopped at Baird's to get some for your hands. Enjoy your day. Love, Maeve and Connor."

Twin daggers of panic and horror drove into Sean as the dull, inevitable thud of the explosion ripped through the air.

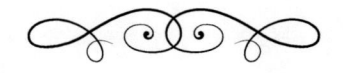

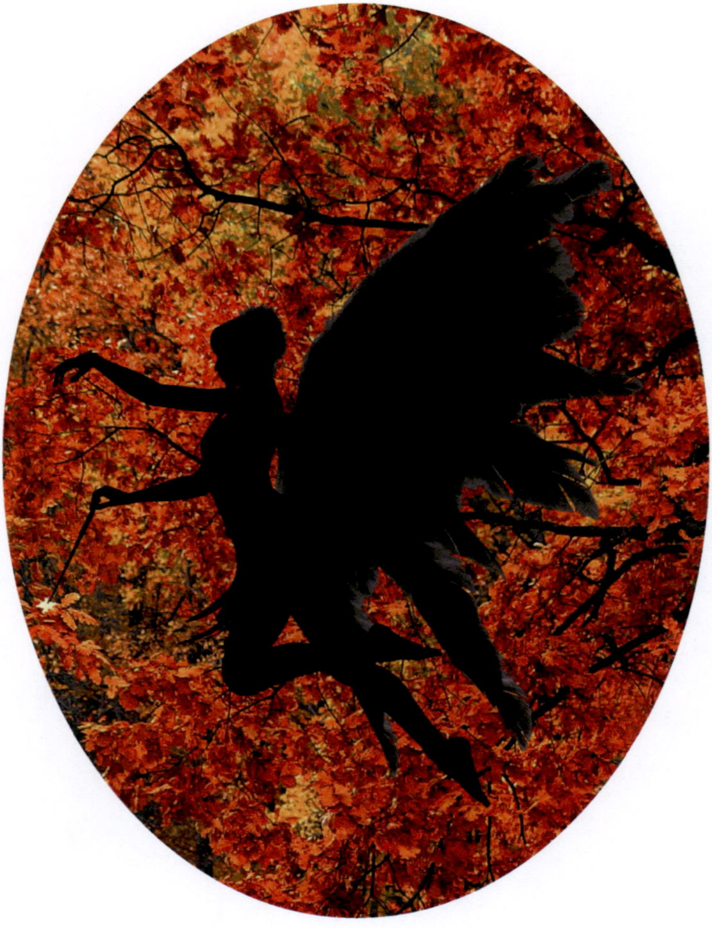

The Fairies' Curse

Jennifer sipped her wine and gazed thoughtfully through her open bedroom window at the grey walls of the little church opposite. The unlikely position of the building always caught her slightly by surprise, for it seemed wedged awkwardly between the houses, as though it had been hammered in, like a gesture of defiance in the face of a torrent of tragedy.

Jennifer sighed. She was glad to be leaving this odd, parochial settlement of mismatched houses and charmless, slogan-ridden footpaths which had been home to her for over twenty-five years. Her relief wasn't confined to the aesthetics of the place either; it was the knowledge that the long fingers of misfortune were not grasping greedily at her throat, as seemed, alarmingly, to be the case for so many of her neighbours.

In a week's time, she would be moving to Belfast, where a teaching job and a flat beckoned towards the future. She drained her glass, and, against better judgement, poured another, before settling down to wait for her boyfriend to arrive and whisk her away from the memory of the stricken faces at today's funeral and her own ancient unease that had risen, unbidden, from deep within.

Her grandmother's words echoed with sinister resonance in her head:

'There's no luck with building on fairy ground. You wait and see.' Jennifer's mother had scoffed at the old woman, wanting her new house completed, but to Jennifer, they were chilling and did not sit easily with her fantasies around the nature of the tiny, exquisite and utterly magical little beings who would dance around their blackthorn trees in the subtle mists of ethereal spring dawns.

Yet the reality was stark: death had stalked the youth of this tiny community like a triumphant bird of prey, from the sudden accident of eighteen-year-old Paul Heasley on his father's tractor, through the heroin overdose of the junkie son of the Robinson family to the slow, inevitable leukaemic tragedy of little Alison from the boisterous family of thirteen in the slow-slung bungalow opposite.

And now, most poignant of all, the death in childbirth of the fragile and beautiful Yvonne Taggart, who was buried in her wedding dress, her tiny stillborn child wrapped protectively in her arms. The whole community had turned out to watch in stunned silence as the tragic little cortège moved slowly up the road and into the grey church. Jennifer would never forget the terrible, anguished eyes of Yvonne's young husband, the bowed grief of her father or the savage blond beauty of her four brothers as they reverently carried the coffin of their only sister along the cracked road in their cheap suits.

The sudden noise of the car horn outside jerked her out of her reverie, making her scramble to get ready. Stephen didn't like to be kept waiting. Moments later, Jennifer was leaning over to kiss him lightly in greeting, but already his eyes were narrow and disapproving.

'What's wrong?' she asked uneasily.

'You know I don't like that dress,' he said flatly, pushing the car into gear. 'We agreed you wouldn't wear it again.'

Jennifer sighed. 'I can change it,' she said quietly.

'Don't bother. We'll be late if you go back in,' he replied tersely. 'Anyway, if you really cared what I thought, you wouldn't be wearing it in the first place.' He paused, eyeing her suspiciously. 'Have you already been drinking?'

That night, Stephen hit Jennifer for the first time. She hid the fact from everyone and drank a little more wine to cope with her secret.

A year later, Jennifer was drinking two bottles of wine each day and was being beaten up regularly. As she lay dying six months after that, with a mind terminally blurred by alcohol and violence, it still didn't occur to her that she was only the latest victim of the fairies' curse.

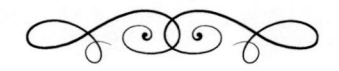

82

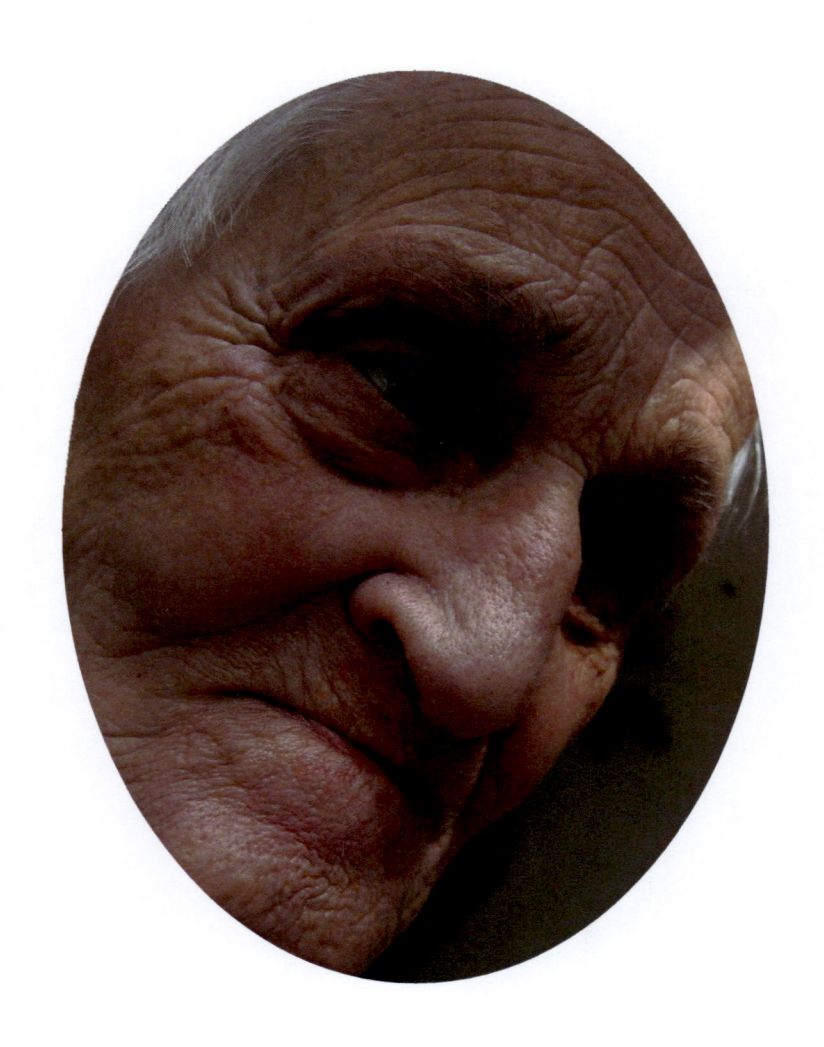

(A Prayer For) A Perfect Death

Let me be old, but still independent,
Let me be sitting by my cheery fire
With the afternoon sun slanting in through the window
Lighting my marigolds in their pretty jar.
I'll finish my tea and my chocolate biscuit
And I'll feel like a nap in my favourite chair.

Let me look around with a sudden great tiredness
And a sense that my work here is done.
Let me know that I've lived with integrity
And that truth was always my goal.
Let me know that my life has had meaning
And reveal to me why I've been here.

Let me be thankful for kindness I've known
Let me forgive all wrong that's been done
Let me have compassion for all living things
Let those whom I love forgive me
For not saying good-bye.
But let them know how to love through my humble example.

As my eyes close in the heat of the fire,
Let me see the perfection in all things.
As sleep drifts seamlessly into another place
And my old soul departs,
Let me know peace.
Let me know God.